AMERICAN
SWAMPS
AND WETLANDS

WILLIAM K SMITHEY

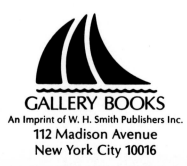

GALLERY BOOKS
An Imprint of W. H. Smith Publishers Inc.
112 Madison Avenue
New York City 10016

Text
William K. Smithey

Design
Clive Dorman

Jacket Design
Claire Leighton

Commissioning Editor
Andrew Preston

Publishing Assistant
Edward Doling

Editorial
Gill Waugh

Production
Ruth Arthur
David Proffit
Sally Connolly
Andrew Whitelaw

Director of Production
Gerald Hughes

Director of Publishing
David Gibbon

Photography
Planet Earth Pictures:
J. Brian Alker 6 *top*, 15 *top*, 22, 24 *top right*, 27 *bottom, center*, A.P.
Barnes 15 *bottom*; Franz J. Camenzind 6 *bottom*, 8 *top*, 11 *top*, 24
bottom; David E. Rowley 4, 10-11, 28-29, 31; Mary Clay 12-13, 12
bottom, 14 *top*, 25 *left*; Richard Coomber 19; Robert D. Franz 16
bottom, 20 *top*, 30; Peter Gasson 16 *top*; Dan Gotshall 13 *bottom
left*; Robert A. Juriet 32; Kenneth Lucas 9, 13 *bottom right*, 20
bottom, 21; John Lythgoe 5 *top*, 14 *bottom*, 15 *top*, 18, 23, 26; Doug
Perrine 5 *bottom*, 25 *right*; Mike Potts 8 *bottom*, 17; Joyce Wilson
7, 24 *top left*, 27 *top*.

CLB 2490
This edition published in 1990 by Gallery Books,
an imprint of WH Smith Publishers, Inc,
112 Madison Avenue, New York 10016.
© 1990 Colour Library Books Ltd, Godalming, Surrey, England.
All rights reserved.
Colour separations by Scantrans Pte Ltd, Singapore.
Printed and bound by New Interlitho, Italy.
ISBN 0 8317 6982 3

Gallery Books are available for bulk purchase for sales promotions
and premium use. For details write or telephone
the Manager of Special Sales, WH Smith Publishers, Inc,
112 Madison Avenue, New York, New York 10016 (212) 532-6600.

CONTENTS

INTRODUCTION

As the environments that combine features of open water and dry land, wetlands fulfil an ancient and indispensable role. The shallow waters of primeval wetlands must have provided the proper balance of moisture, light, warmth and nutrients necessary for early aquatic plants to grow and reproduce. Within these areas of abundant food and nurturing conditions, ancient animal life would have flourished. The calm, muddy shores of ancient wetlands were probably the place where the first aquatic life forms gradually adapted to the opportunities that awaited them on the land.

Throughout the millions of years since living things first solved the problems of a terrestrial existence, wetlands have remained a pivotal part of the earth's biosphere, important in terms of the habitat and the food they provide for wildlife and in terms of the abundance of food they provide for man. The relationship with man has always been an equivocal one, trading the abundant supply of waterfowl and fish against the constant danger represented by poisonous snakes, lurking crocodiles and disease-carrying insects.

The early civilizations that gathered around the delta marshes and flood-plain forests soon discovered that, just as they could harness water to irrigate land too dry for their crops, so they could also drain it from areas that were constantly inundated. With the water removed, the organic-rich muck became extremely rich farmland. As long as three thousand years ago, Mediterranean city states drained marshes and lakes for conversion to cropland.

While the actual mechanisms that connect wetlands with disease have only become understood in the last century, the association between marshes and insect-borne disease had certainly been made in historical times. Through a combination of draining wetlands to promote agriculture and to eradicate disease, wetlands have been dramatically reduced as civilization has expanded. European wetlands of significant size have been reduced to pitifully small numbers and only in Scandinavia and the Soviet Union do significant European wetlands remain.

California's last wild river, the Smith River (below) is located in far northwestern California. The Big Cypress Swamp National Preserve (facing page top) in the Everglades is inhospitable to man but a prime habitat for wildlife. The Everglades (facing page bottom) are an extensive wetland region located in southern Florida.

MAN AND NORTH AMERICA'S WETLANDS

In North America, the early European colonists harvested ample provisions from the salt marshes that surrounded their first coastal colonies. Ironically, they imported the same pathogens that had become synonymous with Old World wetlands. With their ever-increasing population and new, imported diseases, the New World wetlands were doomed.

As settlement moved westward, wetlands were routinely drained for agriculture. The tallgrass

Though much of Florida's Everglades (facing page top) remains largely intact, the impact of civilization has changed the natural patterns of flood and drought. Facing page bottom: the McNeil River during the salmon run, when grizzly bears gorge on the shoals of fish returning to their breeding grounds. Below: a bull elk in velvet.

prairies and lower Great Lakes region, historically the sites of the richest wetlands, disappeared so early that little is known of their natural history. Only a legacy of creatures now either rare or disappeared remains; these include the Carolina parakeet, whooping cranes and trumpeter swans. Ninety percent of the vast tule marshes that once covered the great Central Valley of California have been drained to make way for agricultural crops. Within this vast area the grizzly bears, pronghorn and elk have been replaced by crops such as rice and cotton and by fruit orchards. In all, Americans have drained or filled more than one half of the original wetlands in the conterminous United States, either to make way for agriculture, urban development, dams, canals, harbors, highways, or for other reasons.

FRESHWATER WETLAND TYPES

RIVERS AND STREAMS

Many natural phenomena are easily recognized as being cyclical in character. Perhaps less obvious is the way water is endlessly cycled, evaporating mainly from the ocean and falling on the earth as precipitation. Eventually the water is collected by the vast and intricate system we call streams and rivers to be delivered, with gravity as the motive force, back to the ocean.

There is no typical river or stream, since each is the product both of the terrain along its path and of regional weather patterns. The wildlife of these dynamic systems is influenced by many factors, including water temperature, rapidity of flow and amount of oxygen. A snow-fed, rapidly moving mountain stream, aerated as it tumbles through

Fed by melting snow, the Yellowstone River cuts a classic, V-shaped swath as it forms the Grand Canyon of the Yellowstone (right), Yellowstone National Park. As rivers reach the ocean they slow, dropping their accumulated sediment. The Yukon River of Alaska forms a huge delta (below) as it enters the Bering Sea.

rapids and riffles, is typically rich in oxygen. In contrast, a slowly moving river, warming as it makes its way to the sea, holds less oxygen. Whether quick or leisurely, current is the inescapable fact of river and stream life.

Fast-flowing streams require special strategies. Some animals simply avoid the current, living behind rocks or in the stream bed. Stoneflies spend part of their life cycle as streamlined nymphs, attached to rocks and feeding on algae. Other species, such as the brook trout or the rainbow trout, are supremely adapted to life in fast currents, being streamlined and instinctively pointing upstream while hunting for food. The extra oxygen present in cold water allows this energetic lifestyle.

The American dipper is a bird of clear, fast-flowing streams with rapids. It uses its short wings to swim to the bottom where, in the face of seemingly overwhelming currents, it walks along the bed feeding on the larvae of caddis flies, stoneflies, mayflies, aquatic worms and even small fish.

As streams gather to form rivers, they widen and deepen. The slower water warms up and its oxygen-holding capacity decreases. Slow-water fish, in contrast to their fast-water counterparts, tend towards a flattened body shape and are usually less muscular. Their many different types include largemouth bass, yellow perch and pike.

Belted kingfishers are common birds along North American rivers. The kingfisher is supremely adapted for diving after fish, with its oversized head and neck built to absorb shock, and a sharp bill engineered to grip slippery prey.

The sleek rainbow trout (below) is found in swift streams, while the northern pike (bottom) is adapted for life in lakes, or large rivers with slow currents.

LAKES AND PONDS

Freshwater lakes and ponds are simply variations on a theme; both are inland bodies of water, either natural or man-made. Ponds are usually smaller as well as shallower, and they have temperatures that vary little from the surface to the bottom. Lakes are larger and deeper, and because of this, the temperature and the distribution of water vary throughout the year.

As water warms, it becomes lighter, and as it cools, it becomes heavier. As a result, in a typical lake water forms layers separated only by temperature. The extent of this layering often shows annual patterns, being pronounced in the winter and summer and breaking down in the spring and fall. The strong summer stratification results in very little mixing between layers. Each fall, the upper layer cools more rapidly than the deeper layer, eventually becoming more dense and sinking below it. This fall overturn is an important event, moving oxygen into the deep water and bringing nutrients to the surface.

Lakes are most common in areas that were once subject to glaciation. The states of Minnesota, Michigan and Wisconsin each contain

thousands of natural, glacially formed bodies of water. In Florida and Louisiana sinkhole lakes, which were created as the underlying limestone dissolved, are especially common. Many of the mountain lakes of the west are of glacial origin, while a few, notably Oregon's Crater Lake, have formed in extinct volcanoes.

Spring marks the beginning of considerable activity in northern and alpine lakes (right). Along the shallow shore of a pond or lake, thickly vegetated marshes (below) provide suitable habitats for birds such as red-winged blackbirds and marsh wrens. The open water beyond is used by ducks.

INLAND MARSHES

Inland freshwater marshes exist throughout the United States and can form in any basin where water remains long enough for those plants that can tolerate standing water to become established. The amount of water in a marsh can range from enough merely to soak soil to standing water several feet deep.

THE MARSH ECOSYSTEM

With ample sun and copious water, plants grow in profusion throughout a marsh. Their fruits and foliage provide food and shelter for the wide variety of marsh inhabitants. Algae, which use the energy of sunlight to grow and multiply, are the basic crop of a marsh. Zooplankton, made up of various aquatic insects, crustaceans and tadpoles, graze on algae. Fish then feed on the zooplankton and they are in turn eaten in by larger fish, birds, snakes and turtles.

Grasses, bulrushes and cattails grow collectively in the shallower portions of a marsh. These are tall, slender plants that adhere to the soft mud of the marsh bottom via their extensive roots and underground stems.

In somewhat deeper water, aquatic species, such as reeds and wild rice, predominate. Plants that require standing water, such as floating water lilies and submerged aquatic plants, are found here as well. In the southern United States the water hyacinth, an exotic import from South America, may be abundant.

In marshes deep enough for open water to form, underwater plants, such as water celery and bladderwort, take over. To supplement the meager energy to be obtained from the sunlight that manages to make its way through the murky pond water, bladderworts capture aquatic insects using trapdoors contained in air sacs, or bladders.

Grasses (above) typically grow flowers on the ends of long stalks and use the wind to carry and distribute their pollen. The marsh marigold (left) grows in wet places high in the mountains, often blooming very close to receding snowbanks. The leaves and flowers of the water lily (right) float on the quiet waters of ponds. The stomata – tiny openings on the surface through which the plant exchanges gases – are located on the upper surface of the leaf, rather than the lower surface as in most land plants. Brightly colored crayfish (far right) are freshwater relatives of marine crabs, lobsters and shrimps and feed mainly on aquatic plants, though they also take insect larvae, worms, water snails and tadpoles.

MARSH WILDLIFE

The muskrat is a large mouse that is a common resident of the flooded marshlands where cattails are plentiful. Its many adaptations to aquatic life include waterproof fur, a flattened tail and webbed feet. Muskrats build their houses of aquatic plants piled on a foundation of mud, branches and other debris. As they harvest the plants for their house, they create an open water moat that protects them from land-based predators.

Muskrats consume large amounts of aquatic vegetation, including wild rice and cattails. They will also eat freshwater mussels and crayfish. Each autumn, before their upper stalks die back, cattails store nutrients in horizontal stems called rhizomes. While the stored starches are intended to fuel the cattails' growth the following spring, they are also a major food source for muskrats. The muskrat's preference for cattails has the secondary benefit of clearing cattail thickets, thereby opening up clear-water landing sites for migratory waterfowl.

The American bittern is a master of camouflage, its plumage and even bill color blending with the vertical stalks and shadows of the cattail marshes where it lives. With its bill held skyward, paralleling the vegetative patterns, the bittern will even move with the cattails as these sway. The bittern's camouflage is effective both for defensive purposes and when stalking prey.

Other secretive marsh birds include the marsh wren, which inhabits areas deep within the tangled cattail growth, and eats mainly insects, thus helping to keep the inevitable wetland insect population under control. At four feet in height, the great blue heron is easier to find, but can still be overlooked as it stands stock-still along the shore waiting for a fish to swim nearby.

Even as marshlands disappear, one wetland bird, the red-winged blackbird, has thrived. In the fall, when it reaches its peak population, it is the most numerous land bird in North America. While red-winged blackbirds are closely associated with marshes, they are probably an upland species that later adapted to take advantage of the seasonally abundant food of a marsh. Moving between upland fields, to feast on grain and seeds, and marshes, with their abundant insects, has been the key to their success.

Marshes are the favorite habitat of ducks, both as stopping-off points during migrations and as breeding grounds. Marsh ducks can be divided

Muskrats (facing page top), which are aquatic rodents, are found throughout much of North America. Facing page bottom: the secretive American bittern. Above: the great blue heron, which feeds on small mammals, reptiles and small birds, and (below) a ruddy duck, a bird that seldom flies, preferring to escape danger by diving or hiding.

into dabblers, which feed in shallow water, and divers, which feed in the deeper waters of marshes, lakes and ponds. Mallards, pintails, northern shovelers, and gadwalls are dabblers, and can be easily identified as they tip up their tails to feed on aquatic animals and plants. Because they have to navigate under water, diving ducks have legs that are shorter and placed further back on their bodies than those of dabbling ducks. Diving ducks include canvasbacks, redheads and ruddy ducks.

Snapping turtles use their algae-covered shells and dull coloration as camouflage while they wait for fish and other aquatic animals to wander by. When prey is near, they quickly extend their neck and open mouth forward, creating a suction that helps them to capture their prey.

Other turtles, such as the mud turtle, are scavengers, animals that eat nearly everything the marsh has to offer. Once sufficiently warmed by the sun, they hunt frogs, fish and tadpoles and also graze on plant stems and algae.

The mud turtle (above) is active from April to October. During droughts it may move overland or burrow into mud and remain dormant. The male mallard duck (below left) is the more colorful of the sexes. Mallard are the ancestors of the common white domestic duck.

Sedge Meadows

Where the ground is no longer moist enough for a cattail marsh, such as in old lake beds, sedge meadows can appear. Sedges persist in areas with occasional floods but without a constant covering of water. As is often the case when two different habitats are mixed, the part terrestrial and part aquatic nature of a sedge meadow results in a rich sweep of wildlife.

The two-foot-high sedge blades make good cover for small rodents, including arctic shrews and meadow voles, which forage for seeds and insects. Foraging birds, such as Virginia rails, sora, swamp sparrows, and snow buntings, are also attracted to the cover and abundant seed supply of a sedge marsh. When spring rains inundate the marsh, dabbling ducks, such as mallards, northern shovelers and blue-winged teal, stop to rest and feed.

The abundant rodents of the marsh and its surrounding area inevitably attract predators, and none are more tireless hunters than the northern harrier. Harriers spend forty percent of the day flying low across the terrain, constantly watching and listening for prey. They can cover up to one hundred miles a day in search of rodents, shrews, rabbits, frogs and snakes. At night the short-eared owl, equipped with ultrasensitive eyes and ears, emerges to hunt similar prey.

Short-eared owls are crow-sized birds that can be identified by their habit of hovering while hunting.

Bogs

Bogs are unique wetlands, characterized by cold, stagnant water and thick carpets of sphagnum moss. Many bogs are ice-age remnants, glacially sculpted low spots harboring remnant species typically found farther to the north. Other bogs may form in ponds or hollow pockets, where cold air and water collect. They are most common in the glaciated parts of North America, with large complexes present in northern Minnesota. They are also found in the western mountains, the Pacific Northwest, throughout the Appalachians and south as far as the Gulf Coast.

Because the stagnant water of a bog is acid and cold, few things can survive there, even those life forms responsible for decomposing plant remains. As a result, nutrients that are typically recycled by decomposition are left locked up in plants for decades. The tea-colored water characteristic of bogs results from the continuous "steeping" of the preserved remains of dead vegetative matter.

Sphagnum moss is one plant that does thrive in mature bogs, growing as a deep, spreading mat that traps up to twenty-five times its own weight in water. Sphagnum contributes to the stagnant nature of bogs by limiting water circulation and by preventing sunlight from penetrating and warming the lower levels of the bog.

Where sufficient sphagnum accumulates, small evergreen shrubs, such as leatherleaf, can take root. Leatherleaf is one of several evergreen shrubs related to rhododendrons that can tolerate the acid environment. Although perched on the water's surface, the leatherleaf, along with some other bog plants, has developed adaptations to prevent water loss that are similar to those of desert plants. To avoid thrusting their roots into the chilly bog water while their leaves bask in far warmer conditions, these plants are adapted to use every drop of water efficiently.

Some bog plants supplement their nutrient-poor environment by capturing and digesting insects. Pitcher plants use fragrance to attract insects, which then fall into the throat of the plant where their escape is blocked by downward pointing hairs. Eventually they drown in the bottom of the

The northern pitcher plant (this page) bears a large, solitary flower on a leafless stalk. The pitcher plant's highly modified leaves are used to trap insects, which provide the plant with a source of scarce nitrogen. Facing page: highly acidic bogs resist the transition to forest.

plant in a mixture of rainwater, enzymes and bacteria. This digestive broth liquefies the insects and the resulting nutrients are absorbed by the plant. A different approach is taken by the sundew, which catches insects in sticky glandular hairs displayed as a rosette. Once trapped by the sticky hairs, the insect is digested by enzymes and the nutrients are absorbed by the plant.

Black bears visit in the fall, feeding on cranberries and blueberry bushes. Residents include burrowing rodents, such as the Arctic shrew and the northern bog lemming, which use the dry, upper portion of the sphagnum mat. They are hunted in turn by short-eared owls and great gray owls. Fish cannot survive in bog waters, but amphibians such as the northern leopard frog and the wood frog are present, especially during the breeding season.

Birds, such as sparrows and warblers, build ground nests on the open bog. During the spring and summer, palm warblers build nests on clumps of sphagnum moss. Connecticut warblers and Lincoln's sparrows also frequent bogs, while an unusual wood warbler, the northern waterthrush,

searches the water's edge for insects.

Some bog residents are endangered. The pine barrens tree frog is threatened by destruction of habitat, and the Muhlenberg's turtle is in trouble through being gathered by collectors because of its distinctive pattern and color.

VERNAL POOLS

Vernal pools form as winter rains fill shallow depressions that are underlain by impervious hard clay. These conditions are common in certain parts of California along broad, flat mesas or tablelands. Containing shallow standing water for three months of the year, followed by a gradual drying out and then drought, this habitat supports a unique succession of plants. In the spring, as the pools evaporate, a succession of wildflowers grow along the shores of the shrinking pools.

In addition to residing in bogs, great gray owls (facing page top) are found in boreal and dense coniferous forests. Facing page bottom: the leopard frog, which is primarily nocturnal, and (below) tiger salamanders, which, like all amphibians, must return to the water to lay their eggs.

Many of the common grassland species in California are not native, but were brought to North America with the introduction of cattle and sheep from Europe. These imports often out-compete native species. Because of their peculiar cycle of wet and dry conditions, vernal pools are nearly free of these unwanted imports – the pools are simply too wet for true terrestrial plants, while aquatic species cannot survive the temporary nature of the pools. As a result, ninety percent of the vernal pool flora are native and many are endemic, limited to the vernal pool habitat.

The Jepson Prairie Preserve, near Sacramento, California contains one of the world's largest vernal pools. Several rare species are found here, including the California tiger salamander. Two species, solano grass and the delta green ground beetle, are found nowhere else on earth.

THE GREAT SOUTHERN SWAMPS

Early in the history of the United States, while the National Parks of Yosemite and Yellowstone were being established in order to preserve their unique scenery, the great swamps of the Everglades and the Okefenokee were being sold for pennies per acre. These areas only exist in any form today because of the difficulties of draining them. The protection that has finally been afforded these remnant wetlands is a direct result of their conspicuous inhabitants, waterfowl and wading birds – species prized by hunters.

The term swamp is a nebulous one, a phrase conjuring up an image of mud, water and forbidding inaccessibility. This is both true and untrue of the Okefenokee, which is a peat-filled bog – an immense slow-running body of water,

Trees found in the southern swamps include the royal palm, slash pine and wild pine. The growing human population along the Florida coast threatens the water supply vital to the survival of these wetlands.

much of it held in its sandy bottom, a remnant of the ancient sea. The sluggish flow is impeded by cypress trees, sphagnum moss, shrubs in dense thickets and occasional islands. The Suwannee River drains most of the Okefenokee into the Gulf of Mexico.

The Everglades occupy the southern tip of Florida, and constitute a low, flat area of poor drainage – a sea of grass dotted with low islands. With up to sixty inches of rain each year, the interior of the Everglades remains underwater most of the time. As the terrain falls at only two to three inches per mile, water drains slowly and imperceptibly southward toward the Gulf of Mexico. The Everglades are located just west of the densely populated coastal cities of Miami and Palm Beach; as a result they have been dramatically modified by man. Originally covering much of the southern tip of Florida, the Everglades now consist of a belt that is fifty miles wide by one hundred miles long, extending south from Lake Okeechobee to the tip of Florida.

THE OKEFENOKEE SWAMP

The Okefenokee is not a large place by United States wilderness standards. Located mainly in southeastern Georgia, with a small part extending into northwestern Florida, it covers 681 square miles. It was formed more than 250,000 years ago, a time when the Atlantic Ocean extended seventy-five miles inland from the present Georgia coast. As the sea retreated, it formed a sandbar, leaving behind a shallow, sandy-bottomed depression, now known as the Okefenokee. The Okefenokee, surrounded by civilization, has survived a century spent trying to drain and wreck it. Despite man's persistent intervention, its plants and animals have prevailed and it remains as wild a place today as anywhere on earth.

The Okefenokee Swamp is dominated by the bald cypress.

THE REALM OF THE REPTILE

No animal matches the primeval atmosphere of the Okefenokee as perfectly as the American alligator. The first explorers of the American South found them in incredible numbers. Hunted for their skins and the victims of widespread habitat destruction, alligators were once in danger of extinction. Now protected, they have made a dramatic comeback.

Alligator females build a nest as clever as any in nature. They begin by clearing a site, tearing out or trimming the vegetation with their substantial jaws. With these clippings and other aquatic vegetation they build a cone-shaped mound. Between twenty-five and sixty eggs are laid at the top of the mound, packed in mud and more aquatic plants. As it decomposes, the pile of vegetation gives off heat, which incubates the eggs. The

---

Below left: the river otter, an animal adept at hunting fish. Adapted to life in the water, it is also at ease on land, where it runs fairly well. Raccoons (below) are common throughout the United States wherever water is found. Bottom: the impressive jaws, teeth and claws of the American alligator.

hatchlings emerge after nine weeks. Temperature control is critical not just for hatching the eggs but also for determining the sex of the alligator hatchlings. If the nest is cooler than optimum, the eggs will hatch as females, while a warmer than optimum nest results in males. In a properly maintained nest, with the temperature well regulated, the sexes will be equal; this is the case in the vast majority of nests.

Alligators form deep-water pools, called "gator holes", excavating new holes or enlarging existing ones with their powerful snout and tail. Over time, a characteristically dense thicket of shrubs grows in the mulch that surrounds these holes. Alligators keep the holes free of vegetation, making them attractive to resident wildlife, including fish and frogs as well as birds and mammals – all of which become part of the alligator's diet. In spite of their prime inhabitant, these holes also attract visiting wildlife, including raccoon, river otter and water birds.

Emitting sounds that vary from low grunts to barks, frogs and toads are the most numerous and the noisiest amphibians in the swamp. The pig frog, which grows to about five inches in length, is a favorite prey of the alligator. Disregarding the standing water that surrounds it, the oak toad mates and lays its eggs in the temporary ponds that form on the land after spring rains.

Snakes are also plentiful, with most becoming active at night. Southern swamps are home to the venomous cottonmouths and rattlers as well as other, more benign water snakes. The cottonmouth is pugnacious, inevitably holding its ground by rearing its head and gaping its mouth, revealing the pure white inside that gives the snake its name. Several nonpoisonous water snakes resemble the cottonmouth, but are always more timid. The nonpoisonous brown water snake is most frequently mistaken for the cottonmouth. It is a skilled swimmer, feeding on frogs and fishes caught among shoreline vegetation.

There are three rattlesnakes in the Okefenokee, the pygmy, the canebrake, and the eastern diamondback.

OKEFENOKEE BIRDS

Even for the earliest explorers the ivory-billed woodpecker was a rare sight, a reward for having journeyed into the most remote part of a swamp. As the old-growth swampy forests this woodpecker requires were cut down, the bird disappeared. While it is unlikely that any still exist within the United States (there are reliable reports that a few survive in Cuba), the trackless wilderness of the central Okefenokee is the best and last hope.

The prothonotary warbler is a characteristic bird of the southern swamplands. Unlike most other warblers, it nests in tree holes. The anhinga is common in southern swamps, where it is also known as the snakebird because it submerges its body when swimming, leaving only its head and long neck visible above the water.

Water snakes (below left) are live-bearing and can be found in both saltwater and freshwater habitats. Below: a female anhinga regurgitates partially digested fish to its nestlings.

THE EVERGLADES

The Everglades once covered one and a half million acres. Now, served by extensive drainage canals built to convert the land to agricultural use, and by other elaborate water-control systems used for flood and irrigation control, their size and character have been much modified. Fortunately, part of the central Everglades remains intact and a sample of this unique subtropical wetland is protected by the Everglades National Park. Even within the national park, however, man's manipulation of the natural water cycles of the southern Florida area has seriously threatened the Everglades ecosystem.

At its heart the Everglades remain what the native Seminole Indians called "Pa Hy-Okee," or grassy waters. They form a subtropical area where species from the North and South mingle. Jamaican saw grass blankets the heart of the glades. Saw grass can easily grow to ten feet in height and, because it spreads aggressively using underground stems, it can form pure stands.

Two types of islands are interspersed among the saw grass. Willow heads form in depressions where wind-borne willow seeds establish themselves during a dry period. As the trees grow and become established, organic matter

accumulates around their bases, allowing other trees, such as bald cypress or redbay, to become established. Tropical hammocks, in contrast, form on elevated ground one to three feet high. Hammocks are dominated by tropical trees, including royal palm, gumbo-limbo and mahogany.

The inhabitants of these tree islands include orchids and epiphytes, plants that take root in the tree canopy. While living among the treetops frees epiphytes from competition with traditional ground dwelling plants, it does expose them to great extremes of drought and humidity. They have adapted to drought in various ways, which include collecting rain in urn-shaped leaves. These tiny pools are used by tree-climbing species for drinking and, in the case of mosquitoes and some tree frogs, as breeding puddles.

Tinkering with the Everglades water system has exaggerated the effects of natural droughts. Wood storks require hundreds of pounds of fish to fledge their young successfully. Natural droughts in the Everglades concentrate fish in shallow pools, turning the potentially energy-intensive task of finding large numbers of fish into one of simply finding a shrinking pond full of food. However, changes in the Everglades yearly water cycle extend the effects of droughts and actually reduce the number of fish.

The snail kite, a bird that relies on the tiny apple snail as its staple food, is particularly hard hit by prolonged droughts. Apple snails live submerged in shallow pools, traveling to the surface only to breath, feed or lay eggs. During these brief trips to the surface the snail kite uses its specially adapted beak to snatch and eat them. Droughts now destroy the ponds the snails live in, severely affecting the kites in turn.

The mink is the opportunist of the weasel family. Combining the long, thin body of a weasel, a skunk-like ability to release musk and the webbed feet of an otter, the mink is well adapted to wetland life. Its diet is equally eclectic, and depends on the season or habitat. In summer, mink consume fish, frogs, snakes, muskrats, mice, chipmunks and birds. During winter and in colder climates, they eat rodents such as voles, and rabbits.

Facing page: moss drapes from a cypress tree in the Everglades of Florida. Wood storks (top right) usually nest on large cypresses surrounded by water. Tree frogs (center right) are found in trees, such as tupelos, that grow in standing water. Also called air plants, epiphytes (right) grow on trees.

THE TROUBLE WITH DUCKS

There are four migratory flyways in the United States – the Pacific, the Central, the Mississippi and the Atlantic – utilized by North American duck populations. Because of the loss of habitat both in their wintering grounds and along these migratory routes, ducks have recently suffered sharp declines in their populations.

The Pacific flyway has the greatest problems.

Some ninety percent of the wetlands along this route have been destroyed for agricultural uses. Agricultural runoff, accumulating in the few remaining wetlands, has exposed waterfowl to toxic pollutants including selenium and organic pesticides. One major waterfowl area, the Kesterson National Wildlife Refuge in California's San Joaquin Valley, has been drained because

28

toxic selenium concentrations carried by irrigation runoff caused birth defects in hatchlings.

Vying with the Pacific flyway for the greatest number of ducks, the Mississippi flyway is suffering from rapidly dwindling habitat at its southern end. As Arkansas and Mississippi lose bottomland forest to agriculture, the coastal marshes of Louisiana are being lost at a rate of fifty thousand acres per year. Despite this rapid loss, Louisiana still retains forty-five percent of the remaining marshes in the lower forty-eight states.

While many species of bird are declining in number, in eastern Canada the snow goose population is increasing at a rate of over one hundred thousand each year. These birds graze in the fields and marshes of Pacific coastal areas all winter, migrating to breed in the far north.

In contrast to the National Forest and National Park systems, the national legislation concerning wetlands evolved slowly and in a piecemeal fashion. Because protection was late in coming for the remains of America's underappreciated wetlands, two notable species, the whooping crane and the trumpeter swan, would undoubtedly have become extinct, except that they nest in inaccessible areas. In fact, the whooping cranes' nesting grounds in Canada's Wood Buffalo National Park were not located until the 1950s.

The whooping crane, once a wide-ranging species distributed throughout the North American prairies and east to the Atlantic coastal marshes, reached a low of fifteen individuals in 1941. With numbers that are still dangerously low but slowly increasing, the crane has been preserved by the protection of the its migration route through Oklahoma, Kansas, Nebraska and other states. Captive breeding has also helped to sustain this endangered bird.

As the world's largest swan, the trumpeter swan was denied access to its traditional United States breeding grounds by development and agriculture. Additionally, killing for meat, skin and feathers hastened their decline. By the 1930s, the trumpeter was near extinction and only full protection enabled its recovery. Today it has been successfully reintroduced into parts of its former range.

Trumpeter swans begin nesting in late April. Using the masses of bulrushes, reeds, grasses and sedges, the nest is built on muskrat houses, beaver lodges or along the shore. Adults feed mostly in shallow water, plunging head and neck below the surface to eat the leaves and stems of the aquatic plants that grow on the bottom. They may also use their powerful legs and large webbed feet to dig holes in search of shoots and roots. Hatchlings eat aquatic crustaceans and beetles, switching to aquatic plants by five weeks of age.

Trumpeter swans display with mutual spreading and raising of wings (facing page). Pairs form a long-term bond and nests are often built on muskrat nests surrounded by water. Bears (right) are seasonal wetland visitors, arriving when berries and other foods are plentiful. Overleaf: an elk in Yellowstone National Park. Wetlands are important to visiting animals, such as elk, as well as to the many resident species that are totally dependent upon them.

Wetlands are among the most productive environments on earth. The plants that grow in a salt marsh produce four times the biomass of a modern cornfield. This high biological productivity, the sum of the living output of all the plants and organisms, is due to their proficiency in converting the sun's energy into carbohydrates, the basic fuel of life, and to their efficiency in recycling what is produced. The rhythmic rise of water adds nutrients to wetlands, while its inevitable fall makes these nutrients available.

Wetlands serve as temporary storage basins, lowering flood crests and contributing to groundwater recharge. Replacing wetlands with asphalt and concrete greatly increases the chance of flooding. As flood waters pass through wetlands they slow, losing their load of silt and decreasing erosion.

While some animals, such as deer and bears, are wetland visitors, many other kinds of wildlife, an estimated 200 species of fish and some 150 types of birds, are totally dependent upon the wetland habitat. As this is drained or its source waters are diverted, these animals will decrease in numbers, and some will vanish altogether.

For all their importance, wetlands continue to disappear. While there has been progress toward their preservation, most of the remaining wetland acres, estimated at around ninety-five million in the conterminous United States, are inadequately protected.